God's Heroes
A Child's Book of Saints

Featuring these heroes of faith
and their timeless virtues.

Pflaum Publishing Group
Dayton, OH
Milwaukee, WI

A note to parents and catechists
Faith is a wonderful gift to share with the children in your care. As St. Francis said, "Preach the Gospel. If you must, use words." Indeed, our actions are instructive. And our children are watching!

Children are also watching the heroes of the headlines. True heroes model moral values. Saints model values of our Christian tradition. Read these simple stories with your children. Help them make the faith connection. Sure, they will learn about these particular saints, but the life lessons can go much deeper.

Text and activities by Jean Buell
First and foremost, Jean is a parent who wants her children to grow up in a home filled with faith, hope, and love. She facilitates many worship and learning experiences for children and families. Other titles in this popular series for children include books on the Mass, Bible, rosary, sacraments, and on making faithful choices. All are available from Pflaum Publishing Group.

Cover illustrations by Elizabeth Swisher
Interior design by Jean Buell and Kathryn Cole
Edited by Jean Larkin

Nihil obstat: Reverend Monsignor John F. Murphy, *censor librorum*, September 4, 2005
Imprimatur: †Most Reverend Timothy M. Dolan, Archbishop of Milwaukee, September 8, 2005

Third Printing September 2008

Pflaum Publishing Group
2621 Dryden Road, Suite 300
Dayton, OH 45439
800-543-4383
www.pflaum.com

ISBN 978-1-933178-30-1

God's Heroes

Who are heroes?

Heroes are people you can admire.
They are very, very good at what they do.
- Some have awesome physical skills, like athletes and explorers.
- Some have amazing performance talents, like actors and singers.
- Some have wonderful qualities, like teachers and grandparents.

When you admire people, you are wishing for something. You wish to be like them!

Whose autograph would I like to have?

Who do I sometimes pretend to be?

Heroes are people who inspire you. They show the best of what people can do. And the best includes service to others. If heroes can do it, you can too. Your wish can come true!

In this book, you will meet some heroes of our faith. They are the saints.
- We admire them, and they inspire us in BIG ways!
- They are the real "super heroes." That's because their power comes from love—God's love!
- They share that love with all of us.

Together, we all belong to God's family—the communion of saints. And in this family, there are lots and lots of heroes.
So... who could be YOUR hero?

Who helps me know Jesus?

God's Heroes

Family members show love in special ways. Is your hero someone in your family? We belong to the great big family of God. And our family has a special mother!

St. Mary, Mother of God
Lifetime: First Century • **Feast Day: January 1**

Mary was the mother of Jesus.

Her parents were St. Ann and St. Joachim. They taught her to love God. She listened to God's word. And she waited for God to send a great new leader.

When Mary was a teenager, an angel appeared to her. The angel told her that she would have a baby son. He would become the new leader of God's people. Mary agreed to do what God wanted.

Mary noticed many things when Jesus was born. And she noticed many things while he grew up. They fit with God's word. And they helped Mary understand God's will for Jesus. She taught Jesus the traditions of their faith. And she prepared him to be the leader of God's people.

Years ago, Mary was the mother of Jesus. Now Mary is the mother of God's family. She lives with God forever. She has appeared to people like St. Bernadette and St. Juan Diego. When she appears, she tells us to care for people who are poor.

St. Mary is my favorite because she is the mother of Jesus. She helps the sick people and the poor people. If I become pope, I would want people to call me Pope Mary!
—Julia P., age 9

God's Heroes

St. Mary teaches us to pray with our hearts. First of all, find the name for this way to pray. Add the missing letter to each blank. Then write it in the box on the side. Read the boxes downward. You can pray this way by doing one step at a time.

___ray every day.
___ay attention to God's word.
___ut your trust in Jesus.

___pen y__ur heart. D__n't judge __thers.
___pen y__ur eyes. L__ __k ar__und you.
___pen y__ur ears. Listen, too.

___otice whe__ love is prese__t.
___otice whe__ love seems abse__t.
___ever doubt that God is there.

___ream: *What will make the world a better place?*
___ecide what you can __o.
___o it. This is your mission!

___xplain your dr__am to oth__rs.
___ncourage th__m to h__lp you.
___njoy b__ing J__sus' h__lp__r.

___emember that God loves you.
___eceive God's blessing.
___espond with g__atitude.
Say "Thank you, God!"

The border around these words shows another way to pray with St. Mary. What is it? _____

God's Heroes

Can heroes ask questions? Of course! Think about this: If one student asks a question, then the whole class gets more information. That student is a hero, just like this saint was.

St. Thomas

Lifetime: First Century • **Feast Day: July 3**

St. Thomas was one of Jesus' apostles.

He lived in Galilee. He was probably a fisherman like some of the other apostles. They were Jesus' helpers.

Jesus taught the apostles about God. Sometimes they were confused. They did not understand what Jesus meant. But Thomas asked questions. One day he said, "Lord, we do not know where you are going. How can we know the way?" And Jesus said, "I am the way, and the truth, and the life."

Later, Thomas doubted Jesus' resurrection. He refused to believe when others said that Jesus rose to new life. He had to see for himself. Then he believed. Jesus said, "Blessed are those who have not seen and yet have come to believe."

Thomas was with the apostles on Pentecost. They all were filled with the Holy Spirit. Then they told people about Jesus and the resurrection. And the people began to believe, too.

> I chose St. Thomas because he was an apostle, and he did not believe that Jesus rose from the dead. So Jesus said, "put your fingers in my hands, and put them in my side: and be not unbelieving, but believing."
> — Jake F., age 10

God's Heroes

St. Thomas encourages us to ask our questions. Then Jesus will help us believe with our hearts. And we can help others believe, too. Look at these pictures. Say them out loud. Listen carefully. Believe what you hear! Write each word on the line below it.

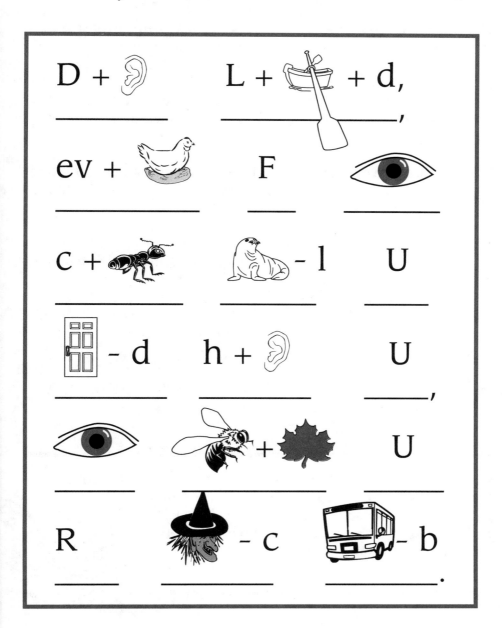

God's Heroes

Do you like to sing? Do you play an instrument? Maybe you and your hero share a musical talent. Music helps us find God in ourselves and in each other. Take note of this saint!

St. Hildegard of Bingen

Lifetime: 1098-1179 • **Feast Day: September 17**

St. Hildegard was a writer of many things, including music.

She was born in Germany. She was the tenth child in her family! As a child, Hildegard was very sick. So she lived in a hermitage, which is a place set far away from people.

The hermitage was located next to a monastery. In fact, it was right next to its church. Hildegard could hear the music coming from the monks at the church.

Hildegard was not highly educated, but she was very creative. She wrote many works of music, poetry, and musical plays. She received many visions from God. God told her to write down everything that she saw in her visions. So she did. Her first work was called "Know the Ways of the Lord." She also wrote about medicines made from items found in nature.

Sometimes Hildegard doubted herself. But she never doubted that her inspirations came from God. She was well respected. She even gave advice to bishops, popes, and kings.

> I like St. Hildegard because she wrote music to bring people closer to God. The time when she lived was chaotic in Europe, especially with the arrival of the plague. She was one of the most creative people of her time.
> —Emily K., age 14

God's Heroes

St. Hildegard shows us that creativity comes from God. Her music is still popular today. Speaking of music, here is a measure of advice from the Bible. Color the bars, or the boxes, that have names of instruments. Then write the rest of the words on the lines below.

	Let	the	piano	word
	of	cello	Christ	dwell
	in	you	trumpet	richly;
	drum	and	with	organ

	gratitude	flute	in	your
	hearts	sing	tuba	psalms,
	hymns,	violin	and	spiritual
	songs	to	guitar	God.

_____

_____

_____

_____

From Colossians 3:16

God's Heroes

Does your hero like adventures? Some people do. They learn to be clever. They learn to make friends. And they learn to trust God. This saint did all that and more!

St. Patrick

Lifetime: 387-461 • **Feast Day: March 17**

St. Patrick was bishop of Ireland.

He was born in Scotland. When he was fourteen, pirates kidnapped him. They took him to Ireland, where the people did not believe in Jesus. There Patrick was a slave and he took care of sheep.

Patrick prayed to God for help. In a dream, God told him how to escape. Patrick went to the coastline. He found some sailors who took him back to Britain.

Patrick became a priest. Years later, Ireland needed a new bishop. In another dream, the Irish people begged Patrick to return. He already knew their language and customs. So he volunteered to go. Patrick became a bishop and went back.

In Ireland, Patrick used a shamrock to teach people about the Blessed Trinity. Many became Christians, but some wanted to kill him. Patrick kept trusting God. He began monasteries, convents, and churches. He worked miracles, and he wrote about his love for God.

> I like St. Patrick because he was kind to the pagans and Druids. He wasn't angry or impatient. I want to be that way, don't you? I want to be a good Christian and be like St. Patrick.
> —Al B., age 11

God's Heroes

St. Patrick helps us know God's great love in the Blessed Trinity. He helps us trust God, too. You can praise God with this prayer. Follow the stems of each shamrock. Write the words inside. Then color the shamrocks—green, of course!

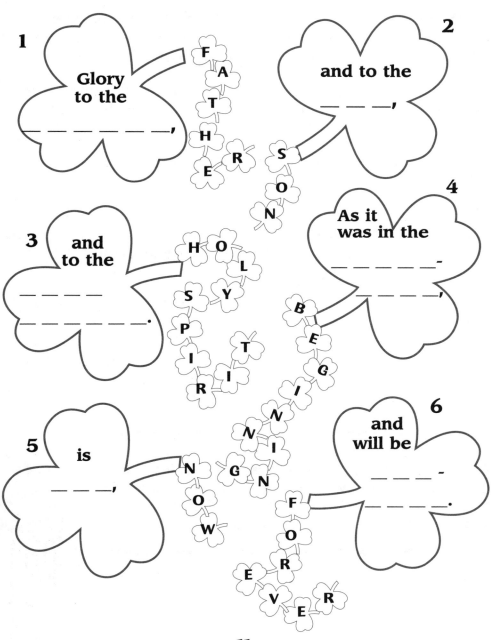

1 Glory to the _____ ,

FATHER SON

2 and to the ___ ___ ___ ,

3 and to the ____ _____ .

HOLY SPIRIT

4 As it was in the _____ - ____ ,

BEGINNING

5 is ___ ___ ___ ,

NOW AND

6 and will be ____ - _____ .

FOREVER

God's Heroes

Do you think of your pet as your friend? Maybe that question makes you giggle! But some children feel a special connection to their pets. And some saints felt a special connection to all of nature.

St. Francis of Assisi

Lifetime: 1181-1226 • **Feast Day: October 4**

St. Francis preached not only to people but to all creatures.

Francis was born in Italy. He grew up in a wealthy family. He was a likeable, easy-going child. His personality helped him serve God. But it took a while!

Francis loved money. He became a businessman. He had lots of friends and lots of parties. They were wild parties!

Francis also loved glory. He wanted to become a knight. So he went to battle. The first time, he was captured. The second time, God told him to go home. So he did. The people thought he failed. They made fun of him.

Francis' life changed. The less money and glory he had, the happier he was. He lived a simple life. He respected everyone.

Francis felt a special connection to nature. All creatures were like his family. All people were, too. He wrote many prayers. Today, people who live as he did are called *Franciscans*.

> St. Francis is a model for seeing God in all things, especially nature. In that way, we find joy and wonder in whatever we touch. Leading a good life full of joy in the Lord, that is St. Francis' special gift to me. —Ken M., adult

God's Heroes

St. Francis reminds us to respect all creation. We all need each other. And we all belong to God. Create your own prayer about creation. Follow the arrows. Check one choice in each section. Then pray your prayer. Erase your checks and create another!

Start Here. If you have a pet, go down. If not, go across.

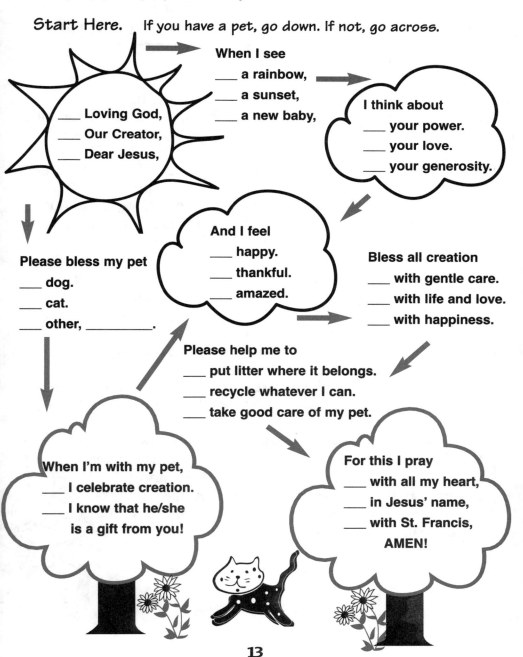

___ Loving God,
___ Our Creator,
___ Dear Jesus,

When I see
___ a rainbow,
___ a sunset,
___ a new baby,

I think about
___ your power.
___ your love.
___ your generosity.

And I feel
___ happy.
___ thankful.
___ amazed.

Please bless my pet
___ dog.
___ cat.
___ other, _____.

Bless all creation
___ with gentle care.
___ with life and love.
___ with happiness.

Please help me to
___ put litter where it belongs.
___ recycle whatever I can.
___ take good care of my pet.

When I'm with my pet,
___ I celebrate creation.
___ I know that he/she
is a gift from you!

For this I pray
___ with all my heart,
___ in Jesus' name,
___ with St. Francis,
AMEN!

God's Heroes

Maybe your hero is someone with lots of clothes and lots of toys. It seems like having lots of "stuff" will make us happy. But this saint discovered true happiness without it.

St. Clare of Assisi

Lifetime: 1194-1253   •   **Feast Day: August 11**

Clare devoted her life to Jesus.

She was born in Italy. She grew up in a wealthy family. As a teenager, she heard about Francis of Assisi. He felt peace and joy. She wanted to feel it, too. So she left home to join him.

Clare and Francis became good friends. He found a home for her and the women who joined her. They chose a simple life. But simple does not mean easy! They had no beds. They wore no shoes. They ate no meat. And they lived in silence and prayer. They were poor but happy. They felt God's love.

Clare was the leader for her group. So she often chose the hardest housework. This inspired the others to trust God.

Clare often prayed to Jesus in the Blessed Sacrament. This devotion saved her group from an attack by soldiers.

Today, many women follow Clare's example. They devote their lives to Jesus. They are called the *Poor Clare Sisters*.

St. Clare was a woman of the Church, deeply in love with Jesus Christ and the Gospel. A woman of compassion and prayer, she saved her sisters from warring armies. She is a woman for our time, full of love and peace.
—Sister Helen, adult

God's Heroes

St. Clare helps us to live simply as Jesus did. Hard work can bring us happiness. Gentle play can bring us joy. Love makes the difference! Try the ideas below. First, unscramble the words. Match them to the pictures. Then, "simply" have fun!

1. akeb some ooksiec
   _____ some _____

2. reda a koob
   _____ a _____

3. ider your ikeb
   _____ your _____

4. pakc a icpicn
   _____ a _____

5. wathc the loudcs
   _____ the _____

6. fyl a ekit
   _____ a _____

7. layp some kclikabl
   _____ some _____

8. ypla some eckchers
   _____ some _____

God's Heroes

Lightly color the squares across these two pages like a checkerboard. Then see if you can answer the questions. Check your answers by reading across the row.

Start coloring here ...➤

Who was the first U.S.-born saint?	St.	God	Elizabeth	mom.
Who was the "apostle to the apostles"?	values	St.	your	Mary
Whose generosity is seen in December?	Jolly	life	Old	bout
Who organized groups to share food and clothing with people who needed them?	Padua	St.	of	Vince
Who saw visions of St. Mary in Mexico?	St.		Juan	exe.
What are "feast days"?	Joachim	days	and	to
What do we celebrate on November 1?	Feast	John	of	uke'
What do we celebrate on November 2?	Baptist	Feast	the	of

Turn this page upside down to finish the puzzle.

n	jobs	Seton	special	What are vocations?
that s	Mag-	actions	dalene	What are virtues?
t.	ideas	Nicholas	important	What are values?
Anth	de	St.	Paul	Which saint will help you find lost items?
go	Katharine		St.	Who spent her own $12 million to help Native Americans?
An	honor	Sts.	saints	Who were St. Mary's parents?
l	Mark	Saints	Matthew	Which saints wrote the gospels?
Jor	All	St.	Souls	Which saint baptized Jesus?

Find a partner and play checkers. Use 12 pennies and 12 dimes for the checkers. Quiz each other. Have fun!

God's Heroes

Does your hero make you laugh? Healthy laughter is fun. It fills our hearts with joy. That is what God wants for us. This saint knew that. He used humor to teach people about God.

St. Philip Neri

Lifetime: 1515-1595   •   **Feast Day: May 26**

Philip was a priest. He was cheerful and likeable.

He was born in Florence, Italy. He grew up in a poor family. He was a "spirited" child. And he was an unpredictable adult!

Philip left home at eighteen. He studied to be a businessman. But he changed his mind. He devoted his life to God instead. So he went to Rome. There he studied religion. But he changed his mind again. He devoted his life to prayer. And he discovered new energy to serve God.

Philip served God in many ways. One way was to help young men. He knew they needed guidance. So he invited them to meetings. The meetings included discussion and prayer. Philip also arranged a big picnic. The group grew and grew.

Philip used humor to help the people in his group. He told jokes. He played pranks. And he helped the people become humble. Then they discovered great ways to serve God. Many people asked Philip to guide them, even other saints!

I like St. Philip Neri because he told jokes. I chose Philip as my Confirmation name because I have a good sense of humor, too. I like to make people laugh.—Brian B., age 15

18

God's Heroes

St. Philip reminds us to be playful. You can brighten the day with a smile or a giggle. Read these jokes out loud. Listen carefully to the underlined words. Write the correct words where there are parentheses. Then do the activities that follow.

1. Knock-knock! <u>Who's there?</u> Dewey. <u>Dewey who?</u>
Dewey want to mix faith and fun? (_____ _____)
Read Psalm 126. Smile ten times today.

2. Knock-knock! <u>Who's there?</u> Allie Lou. <u>Allie Lou who?</u>
Allie Lou praise to God! (_____)
Read Psalm 100. Write your own psalm of praise.

3. Knock-knock! <u>Who's there?</u> Bea. <u>Bea who?</u>
Don't worry, *Bea* happy! (_____)
Read Matthew 5:1-11. Tell what makes you happy.

4. Knock-knock! <u>Who's there?</u> Ken. <u>Ken who?</u>
Ken you say the Greatest Commandment? (_____)
Read Deuteronomy 6:4-9. Make a sign for your door.

5. Knock-knock! <u>Who's there?</u> Sharon. <u>Sharon who?</u>
Sharon care is what we do! (_____ _____)
Read Acts 2:43-47. Tell how you "sharon" care.

6. Knock-knock! <u>Who's there?</u> Hatch. <u>Hatch who?</u>
Hatch who!!! God bless you! (_____)
Read Numbers 6:24-26. Say THIS to someone who sneezes!

God's Heroes

Do you know any firefighters, police officers, or people in the military? They are brave heroes. They keep us safe. And they face dangers, too. So did many saints.

St. Joan of Arc

Lifetime: 1412-1431 • **Feast Day: May 30**

Joan was a teenager who saved her country.

She was born in France. She grew up in a poor family. As a young teenager, she saw a light and heard her name called. Later, she heard the voices of three saints. She listened to them.

At first, the saints helped Joan grow in prayer. She began to help people who were sick or poor. Later, the saints revealed her mission: She was to help save France.

At that time, British forces were invading. Joan met with a general of the French forces. She told him about her mission. He laughed at her. But the saints reassured her. Finally, the generals allowed her to take over.

First, Joan gave the soldiers spiritual guidance. Then, town by town, they won back France. In the end, Joan was captured and sold to the British government. They did not believe that God inspired her mission. So she became a martyr. This means she died for her faith. Years later, they realized she was right.

> I like St. Joan for many reasons. She listened to God and the angels because she believed in them. She knew that they would not deceive her. And she did not fear death. She was a very brave woman. —Elena V., age 11

God's Heroes

St. Joan gives us courage. Some heroes are given awards for their courage. How about you? When do you have courage? Design an award below. Put your initials in one section. Add meaningful symbols to the rest. Then color the medal.

God's Heroes

Maybe your hero is a leader. Leaders make decisions that affect many people. Some saints were leaders who made fair decisions. They were kings, queens, bishops, and popes.

St. Edward the Confessor

Lifetime: 1003-1066 • **Feast Day: October 13**

Edward was king of England. He was a good ruler.

He was a kind and gentle person. People trusted him and believed in him. He was married to a woman named Edith.

King Edward ruled with peace. He solved conflicts by talking instead of fighting. He never said unkind words about anyone. He also ruled with justice. He stopped taxes that were unfair.

He made time for his people. He often stood by the palace gate to meet them. There they gathered around him. He healed people who were sick. And he gave money to people who were poor. Some people say that he gave his ring to a beggar. This shows how much he respected the people who were poor.

And King Edward always made time for God. In fact, he became king on an Easter Sunday! He attended daily worship. He called for many churches to be built and rebuilt. And he let his faith guide everything that he did.

I admire St. Edward because he spent time with his people. All leaders should do that. We should listen. Then we will discover the Holy Spirit at work. —Father Mike, Pastor, St. Edward's Catholic Church

God's Heroes

St. Edward shows us how to be fair leaders. Jesus does, too. Imagine a king and queen of hearts. They follow Jesus. They lead their people with love. What is their rule? Follow the code. Write the letter inside each card. Now follow the rule!

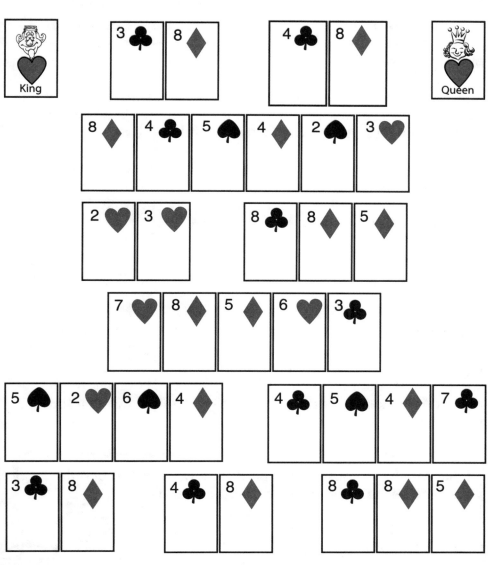

From Matthew 7:12

CODE

2 ♥ = A   3 ♣ = D   4 ♦ = E   5 ♠ = H   6 ♥ = L   7 ♣ = M   8 ♦ = O

2 ♠ = R   3 ♥ = S   4 ♣ = T   5 ♦ = U   6 ♠ = V   7 ♥ = W   8 ♣ = Y

23

God's Heroes

Who takes care of you when you are sick? That person is a special hero. That person helps you feel better from the inside out! Many saints took care of people who were sick.

Blessed Teresa of Calcutta

Lifetime: 1910-1997   •   **Feast Day: September 5**

Mother Teresa helped the poorest of the poor.

She was born in Macedonia and named Agnes Gonxha Bojaxhiu. Her father died when she was young. So her mother began a sewing business. Agnes was active in church.

When Agnes was 18, she joined a convent in Ireland. There she received the name "Teresa," after St. Therese Lisieux. Soon she went to India. Years later, she made her final vows to become a nun. Then she was called Mother Teresa.

One day, Mother Teresa received a calling from God. So she organized a group of helpers in India. They helped the poorest people there are.

The poorest people have no money, no family, and no friends. Many are very, very hungry and very, very sick. They are suffering. When Mother Teresa looked at them, she saw Jesus. When she cared for them, she cared for Jesus, too. This gave them dignity. Today, the Missionaries of Charity continue Mother Teresa's work throughout the world.

I like Mother Teresa because she always made people smile. She had the grace of God in her. One day she gave her lunch to three children who were watching her. I would like to practice the virtue of charity like she did.
— Andrea B., age 12

God's Heroes

Blessed Mother Teresa inspires us to love people who are suffering. That is compassion. Anyone can show compassion any time. Some people show compassion every day. What are their jobs? Find them and circle them below.

```
D O C T O R S A B Z C M
E M O M S V E T S O D I
N U R S E S Y Q U O M S
T P E F G     H I K I S
I R J K L     M N E N I
S I D             E I O
T E A             P S N
S S D O P     Q R E T A
N T S T U     V W R E R
U S T E A C H E R S R I
N C O U N S E L O R S E
S C H O O L N U R S E S
```

Word List

COUNSELORS · MISSIONARIES · SCHOOL NURSES
DADS · MOMS · TEACHERS
DENTISTS · NUNS · VETS
DOCTORS · NURSES · ZOOKEEPERS
MINISTERS · PRIESTS

Do you see a cross in the puzzle? Color it red. A red cross is a symbol of care and compassion. Why do you suppose that is?

God's Heroes

Do you admire a sports player? Successful athletes need physical strength and skills. They also need concentration. This saint concentrated his strength on serving Jesus.

St. Christopher

Lifetime: 3rd century • **Feast Day: July 25**

Christopher was a martyr.

He was born in Canaan. He was also called Offero. He grew up strong and muscular. He traveled. He looked for adventure.

Offero met a man who lived by a dangerous stream. The man told people where they could safely cross it. He also told Offero about God. Offero accepted God. He began to serve others.

Offero was so strong that he could carry people across the stream. One day, he carried a child. The child became heavier and heavier. It took all his strength! Offero discovered that the child was the Christ child. He was heavy because he carried the weight of the world. And Offero helped.

Then Offero became known as Christopher. The name means "Christ-carrier." He is the patron saint for travelers.

There are very few facts about Christopher's life. So he is no longer honored on the worldwide calendar of saints. But he may be honored on local calendars.

I like St. Christopher because, for my First Eucharist, my grandma gave me a chain with his medal on it. Sports players wear this medal. Since I like to play sports, my grandma thought I would like to wear one, too.
—Sam O., age 8

God's Heroes

St. Christopher reminds us to carry Christ wherever we go. Are you on a sports team? If so, you probably play some games at *home* and some *away*. Bring Jesus with you wherever you go. You will always win. How can that be? Travel this maze to find out. Write the words that you find along the path.

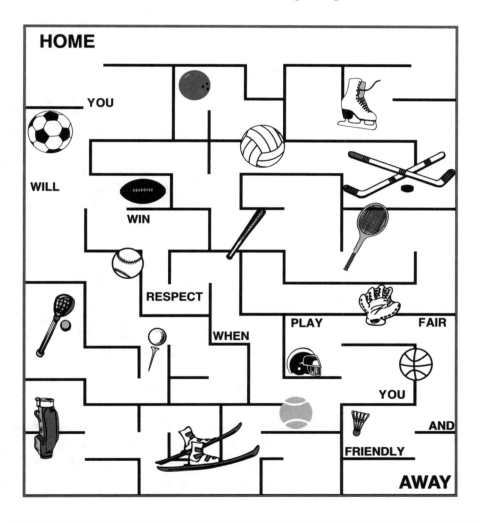

_____

_____

_____

God's Heroes

Maybe your hero is someone who ignores people who are teasing them or putting them down. Can you? You are strongest when you find God's goodness in your heart! This saint did.

Blessed Kateri Tekakwitha

Lifetime: 1656-1680   •   **Feast Day: July 14**

Kateri Tekakwitha is the first Native American to be declared Blessed.

She was born near Auriesville in New York state. Her mother was a Christian in the Algonquin tribe. Her father was a Mohawk. They both died of smallpox when she was only four.

At first, a family friend took care of Kateri. The friend told her stories about Jesus. Then Kateri's uncle adopted her. He was a Mohawk chief. Later Kateri met some missionaries. She became Christian when she was a teenager.

Kateri's uncle was angry with her. The tribe did not approve of her becoming a Christian. They would not give her food. The children made fun of her. They threw rocks at her, too.

Kateri escaped from the tribe. She went to Canada and lived with a Christian tribe. There she could follow her faith. She attended daily Mass. She prayed before the Blessed Sacrament. She cared for people who were sick. And she worked with children.

> I admire Blessed Kateri because she had a strong, unshakable faith, even though the tribe did not approve. She converted to the faith, like I did. She recognized God's truth when she heard it, and it filled her heart with joy.
> — Dorian P., adult

God's Heroes

Blessed Kateri gives us self-confidence. Sometimes people mistreat us. Sometimes they pressure us. But we can stand up for ourselves. How? Change cross words to kind words and loving limits. Follow the clues below.

1. Pray to _____. He loves you very much.

2. Show confidence. Stand up straight. Feel _____.

3. Respect yourself. Choose friends who _____ you, too.

4. Be brave. Ignore cross words. Use kind words.
   Tell yourself good things, like "I have _____."

5. _____ _____ for yourself and your friends.
   Say things like, "No, I won't do that." Or "Don't do that."

6. _____ when you are ready. Jesus will help you.

Word List: courage; forgive; Jesus; respect; speak up; strong

God's Heroes

Are you named in honor of someone? That person's life gives meaning to his or her name. And it gives meaning to your name, too. That person might be your hero!

St. Joshua

Lifetime: 13th century B.C. • **Feast Day: September 1**

Joshua led the Israelites into the Promised Land.

He lived many years before Jesus. They both loved God very much. And both the names Joshua and Jesus mean "God saves."

Joshua was one of the Israelites. They were slaves in Egypt for many years, but God saved them. God gave them freedom. Moses was their leader. He brought them out of Egypt. Then they spent many years in the desert searching for the land God promised them. Joshua was Moses' helper.

After Moses died, Joshua became the new leader. God told Joshua to be strong and courageous. God promised to be with Joshua wherever he went. So Joshua trusted God and set out on his mission to lead the Israelites into the Promised Land. That is where they settled. Joshua reminded them to stay faithful always to God.

Like Joshua, Jesus has a mission. He loves us. He heals us. And he teaches us. Jesus leads us into the "Reign of God." He wants us to stay faithful to God. And he wants us to continue his mission. Saints do exactly that. Every saint's mission is a small part of Jesus' big mission.

> St. Joshua is my favorite saint because his name is the same as mine. He wanted people to have faith in God to go into the Promised Land. —Joshua H., age 9

God's Heroes

St. Joshua, Jesus, and all the saints reassure us of something big: God saves, and we are part of God's plan. We are heroes when we trust God. We are heroes when we serve God, in big ways and small ways. We are saints-in-the-making!

Introducing this hero of faith

Attach or draw your picture here.

I will be known as

Saint _____.

I share God's love in these ways.

At home...   At school...

1.   1.

2.   2.

God's Heroes

Which heroes will be saints?

Heroes live very holy lives. They love God very much. They follow Jesus very closely. They are admired long after they have died.

People may wonder if a certain hero is a saint. To begin making that decision, a bishop makes sure the stories about the hero's life are true. If they are, he gives his information to the Vatican, and the official process starts.

First, the Vatican decides if the hero's life is holy enough for sainthood. If it is, the title "Venerable" is then used with the hero's name. Venerable means holy or worthy of great respect.

Second, there must be a miracle credited to the hero. That means the hero, after death, did something wonderful in answer to people's prayers to him or her. Then the hero is "beatified," and "Blessed" is used before his or her name.

Third, there must be a second miracle credited to the hero. Then the hero is "canonized" and has the new title of "Saint."

After all these steps, the Church is certain that heroes live with God forever. We celebrate their lives. We tell their stories. And we are inspired to be heroes, too. Who knows? Maybe someday, you or your hero will be known as a saint.

But for now... **Which saints will be your heroes?**